SOU...
The Life of ...hi

by
Lucy Jane Bledsoe

Marjorie L. Kelley, Ed.D.
Educational Designer

Quercus Corporation
2405 Castro Valley Boulevard
Castro Valley, California 94546

COVER PHOTO: (Wide World)

Printed in the United States of America.
ISBN: 0-912925-82-5

Contents

1

The Father
of 400,000,000

The year was 1948. The late afternoon sun had set. But it was still hot—that wet kind of heat. For this was the giant country of India. A snake slid along in the dusty road. Not far behind walked an old man named Mohandas K. Gandhi.

He was a small funny-looking man with ears that stuck straight out. He wore only one piece of cloth. He had no hair. And he was so weak he had to lean on two young girls, one on each side. But the eyes of the world were on this man. He knew the secret to power. He called it *soul force*.

Gandhi walked slowly through a big group of people. As usual, he was going to lead evening prayers in the garden. People tried to touch him as he went by. Many held their hands together in front of their faces. They were asking for the great man's blessing.

In the back of the garden, one man stood alone. His name was Godse. A few yards away, another man nodded to him. Godse moved quickly then. He pushed through a great number of people. He made his way to Gandhi at last. He fell to his knees before him. Gandhi blessed him. Next, still on his knees, Godse pulled out a gun. Three shots rang out. Gandhi, the man 400,000,000 Indians called father and loved dearly, was dead.

Who was this man?

From where did his power come?

Why did people around the world call him father?

What kind of magic did he work?

What in the world was *soul force*?

2

Mohandas Gets Married

In 1882 the British Empire was at its mightiest. The English had spread themselves around the world. They ruled countries in Europe, Africa and Asia. They were rich and powerful. No one, they believed, would ever stop them.

India was the biggest country the British ruled. She was a giant country full of riches. The people, however, were very poor.

In this year of 1882, Mohandas K. Gandhi was riding along in an open wagon pulled by two horses. He and his family were traveling to a small town near the sea. It was the town where Mohandas had been born. Mohandas was only 13 years old. But in three days he would be getting married.

People married very young in India. But even for that country, 13 was young. However, Mohandas' father was not rich. And two other young men in his family were getting married. They could save money by marrying Mohandas off at the same time.

Mohandas hadn't had a very happy childhood. He was so shy he had a hard time talking. And he was very afraid of the dark.

The trip was a long and hot one. It took three days. The wagon hit rocks in the road and threw Mohandas this way and that. But he hardly noticed. He had so much on his mind.

Now he wondered what this girl he was to marry looked like. He thought she would be disappointed when she saw him. Mohandas was very small for his age. And he knew he was not very strong or good-looking. She might even make fun of him.

Mohandas' ears turned red at this thought. More than anything, he hated being made fun of. I won't have it, he said almost out loud. I just won't have it! Already, he was angry with his new wife.

"Hey, watch out! Father, look out!" It was Mohandas' brother yelling. Mohandas looked up at the wagon in which his father rode. It had hit a hole in the road. The whole wagon was tipped to its side. Then it went over.

His father screamed for help. The big wagon lay on top of him. It must have badly broken his legs. Mohandas jumped from his own wagon. He ran to his father.

"The wedding," Mohandas' father gasped. "The wedding must go on."

The horses were dancing on their back legs now. Mohandas ran to get hold of them. They had begun trying to pull the overturned wagon—with his father part way under it!

Mohandas' brothers righted the wagon. The horses were still pawing the ground. Mohandas held onto them so they would not break into a run.

The wagon was fine. But his father was badly hurt. They made a bed for the older man in the back of the wagon. Mohandas couldn't believe it when his father said, "Let's go! We can't be late. The wedding will go on!"

"But father—," he said. Mohandas had thought maybe now they could call the whole thing off.

Mr. Gandhi would have none of it. He said if he was to die, he would do so *after* seeing his sons married. And so they made their way to the town by the sea. And Mohandas K. Gandhi, 13 years old, was married the next day.

3

Meat, Smoke, and Women

Mohandas was born a Hindu. Hinduism is a religion in India. The Hindus believe there are many different castes—or classes—of people. The people in the top caste don't have to work at all. The bottom caste of people are called the untouchables. They have to clean the bathrooms and streets. In Mohandas' day, people in higher castes thought these people were not clean enough to touch.

Mohandas' caste was third down from the top. So he was not rich, but he was not poor either. So far Mohandas had not made much

Mohandas K. Gandhi and his wife Kasturbai, 1915.
(Wide World)

of himself. He had done poorly in school. And he was no good at all in sports. Even now, as a married "man," he was still afraid of the dark.

Mohandas thought of his marriage as a fresh start. In the Hindu religion, a man can order his wife around. Mohandas didn't waste any time in doing that. His home would be one place where his word was the last one. Or so he thought.

His young wife's name was Kasturbai. And Mohandas was pleased to find she was quite pretty. But he was not so happy to find that Kasturbai had a mind of her own.

"I'm going to teach you to read," Mohandas told her. They had only been married a few weeks.

"Oh?" Kasturbai asked, a fire in her eyes.

"Yes," said Mohandas, angry already. "I should think you would want to read."

"Not really."

"Well, I am your husband," said the thirteen-year-old angrily. "And you will do as I say."

Kasturbai only lowered her head.

"Now," Mohandas started out. "This word is . . ."

He worked with Kasturbai on her reading for a few weeks. At the end of that time she hadn't learned a word.

"I won't have this in my home!" he yelled at her. "You are not even trying."

"That is not true," she fired back. "You are a bad teacher."

"You are a bad learner! There's nothing up there in your head!"

Kasturbai turned her back to him and went to her room. When he came in, she was packing her bags.

"What are you doing?"

"I am going home."

"Then go," Mohandas said leaving the room. But he felt a lump when he tried to swallow. Inside he felt sorry. In a funny kind of way, he already loved this girl—even though sometimes she made him so mad. He wanted to be with her every second. And when she was away, he was sick with jealousy. He did not want her out of his sight.

Their families had not really planned for them to be together all the time. Not until they were older. So when Kasturbai got tired of Mohandas, she just went home for a few weeks. This, of course, always made Mohandas more angry. But there was not much he could do about it.

When he was about 16, Mohandas made a good friend. Methab was very different from Mohandas. He was big, strong and good-looking. He did well in sports. And he used strong words. He knew his way around with women, too. He told Mohandas he would teach him how to be a real man.

"For one," he told his friend. "You have to start eating meat."

"But we're Hindu," Mohandas said. "It's against our religion."

"Look," he said pushing a finger at one of Mohandas' thin arms. "Who is big and strong around here? Who in India rules? The English, that's who. A tiny handful of English rule 400,000,000 Indians. And it's also the English who eat meat. You just have to put two and two together. Why don't Indians start eating meat?

We could overcome the English in no time."

"You really think so?"

"Sure," Methab threw a rock to show how strong he was. "How do you think I got this big?"

"You mean you eat meat?"

"Of course."

The next week, Methab and Mohandas bought themselves two big lumps of goat meat. They went to the river where no one could see them. Eating meat was one of the worst things a Hindu could do. When the fire was roaring, they put the meat on to cook. The meat popped as it browned on the fire. Mohandas felt a little sick as he watched.

"Here you go," Methab said with a smile. He had put a stick through the biggest piece of meat. He held it out to Mohandas.

Mohandas ate the meat fast so he wouldn't have to think about it. When he finished, he stood up to go home. He told Methab he felt great. But he really didn't feel well at all.

At home he went right to bed. Kasturbai asked how he was. He didn't say a word to her.

By now she was used to his quick changes in feelings. Mohandas lay awake all night. All he could think about was the goat meat he had eaten. He was sure there was a living soul inside him. Looking back on it years later, he said: "I felt as if a live goat were calling 'Baaa!' inside me."

Mohandas spent a lot of time with Methab. He loved his friend. He learned a lot of new things. Besides meat-eating, Mohandas learned to smoke. He even took things out of his brother's room to sell for money. One time Methab tried to get Mohandas to see other women. But he was too afraid to do that.

Mohandas knew he should soon start thinking about making something of himself. But he was young. He saw no point in rushing it. He had gotten married—wasn't that enough growing up for a while?

Then, one night everything changed at once. Mr. Gandhi had never gotten out of bed since the day his wagon overturned. He had been hurt very badly.

Mohandas had been taking care of his father almost every day. Most evenings Mohandas would sit by his bed and read to him. Or he would rub his feet.

But one night he left his father to go visit with Kasturbai. He had noticed that his father looked very bad that night. But he couldn't stand not seeing Kasturbai. He hated being away from her. And so he went.

Only a few hours later his brother knocked on the door to their room. "Mohandas!" he called. And when he dressed and came to the door, "Our father is dead."

Mohandas thought he would never forgive himself. He was supposed to have been with his father then. In his last hour, he had turned his back.

Then there was more bad news. Some months later, Kasturbai's first child died. Mohandas was sure he was the cause of both deaths. He decided it was high time he did something with his life.

4

The High Life in Great Britain

Mohandas' brother had an idea. Why not send Mohandas to England? He could study to be a lawyer.

No one else thought this was a good idea. Mohandas had tried college in India. In the first year, he failed all his classes. What makes anyone think the boy would do any better in an English school?

Besides that, men in Mohandas' caste did not go to England. His uncles gave a strong *No!* to the idea. In England people ate meat. They smoked. They lived another kind of life—not the kind a good Hindu lived.

Mohandas did not tell them that he already ate meat. He did not tell them that he smoked, either. But he did very much want to go to England.

Mohandas felt he needed a fresh start once again. He knew he could study if he put his mind to it. That is, if he could get away from Kasturbai. They still had a stormy marriage. He acted like a wild man sometimes—because of his jealousy.

By now Mohandas was 19 years old. He and Kasturbai had a son. If for nothing else, he had to make something of himself for his son. Besides, he believed England had the key to power. If he could study there, he would learn their secret.

The old men in his caste still said no. His mother said no. She said England would be his downfall. He would fall into the hands of bad men.

But soon she saw that Mohandas had made up his mind. And his brother was helping by giving him the money. Even when the caste said they'd throw him out, Mohandas would not change his mind. England would make him great. He was sure of it.

His mother cried. For a good Hindu to be thrown out of his caste! He might as well be dead.

"Promise me one thing," she said holding her son's hand tightly. "If you promise, I'll let you go."

"Anything," Mohandas said. He was going anyway. But he'd be so much happier with her blessing.

"Promise you will not touch meat, women or wine."

"But—," Mohandas swallowed hard. "But in England—"

"I don't care about what they do in England. Promise me—or you will go without my blessing."

"I promise, Mother," he said looking down at the floor. He knew at once how very hard this trip would be.

The ship took several days to reach England. Mohandas was still a very shy young man. He stayed in his cabin most of the way.

"Come on, fellow!" said the man who shared his cabin. "You can't live off that dried fruit. Come on up and take your meals with the rest of us."

The man was friendly. He liked this young Indian man. Mohandas saw he was kind. And so he told him about his promise to his mother.

The man threw back his head and roared. "That's a good one!" he laughed. "Well, you're a good son to your mother to give it a try. But take it from me, you'll be eating meat within two weeks. Young man, England is a very different country than India. It's much too cold to not eat meat. As for wine and women . . . well!" The man laughed. "We'll see about that one, too."

There were other reasons Mohandas did not want to eat with the others on the ship. He didn't know how to use the English knives or forks. And he still hated to be laughed at. He felt more comfortable staying in his cabin. He ate the nuts and fruits his mother had packed.

Once in England, Mohandas threw himself into the English way of life. He bought the newest thing in men's suits. He even bought a top hat for evenings out. He paid dearly for a gold watch. He would be sure he was every bit as well dressed as the English.

The young man found himself some rooms to live in. He paid too much for them. But he wanted to live in class. At once he began dancing and music lessons. He even started lessons in how to talk well.

All of this was on his brother's money. He sent the bills home. He knew his family was not well off at all. But he would not let his classmates show him up. He was not a lawyer yet—but he would live like an Englishman, a rich one!

That didn't last long. Mohandas added up how much money he spent each month. The bill was giant. At once he realized he had to give up this high life.

Anyway, he wasn't doing well in any of these classes. He couldn't dance to this English music. And he just wasn't made for fancy talking. The English would have to take him for what he was.

Mohandas moved into one small room. He gave up the dancing and music classes. (He still kept his nice clothes, though.) And he got down to studying what he'd come to England for—law.

Mohandas missed his friend Methab. They'd had such good times together. He thought about his promise to his mother. She had never known what was going on under her own roof in India. She'd certainly never know what he did in a strange land across the sea.

But the young man's own ideas were changing. He really didn't want to eat meat. He joined a group of vegetarians in England. He began to read a lot about food. He began trying different ways of eating.

Some of the things he ate were very strange. For a while he ate nothing but fruit. Another time he tried eating only rice and nuts for a few months. He tried to eat as little as he could, and still stay strong.

His classmates thought this skinny Indian man was very strange. But they all wanted to sit at his table at the school dinners. That way they got his part of the wine.

The years went by quickly. At last Mohandas was doing well in something. He passed all of his classes. After three years in England, he sailed home a lawyer.

He looked for his brother as he stepped off the ship. He felt very proud of himself. He had brought English clothes for Kasturbai and his son. He would have his family dress like the English. And they would get the same kind of respect, too. He looked ahead to a good life of making money.

He saw his brother waving then. He ran to him with a smile. His brother did not smile back, though. His face looked like bad news. He took Mohandas' arm and hurried him home.

"Mohandas," he said when they got there. "Mother is dead."

5

A Job in South Africa

Mohandas was truly heart-broken. In many ways he took after his mother more than his father. His mother had given him his grounding in the Hindu religion. The older he grew, the more he thanked her for that.

When his father died, Mohandas believed he had failed him. At least now, he rested easy. While in England, he had kept his promise to his mother.

Mohandas and his family moved to Bombay, a big city in India. Kasturbai loved the new clothes. They bought a fine house. Mohandas was only 23. But he was doing well for his age.

The surprise came when he began looking for work. Mohandas had always believed in English law. Now he saw that the practice of it was often not fair.

"Sure, Gandhi," another lawyer said to him. "Maybe it isn't fair." They were talking about the way most cases got paid off—behind the backs of the courts. "But it's been that way for years. And it's not going to change for you. Look—that's the way we work here. It would be a good idea if you found a way to fit in."

Gandhi tried. But he wasn't going to take money to push a case one way or another. And like the man said, no one was going to change for him. So as it happened, no one gave Gandhi any jobs.

At last he was given a chance. He got a case—a very small one that was not very important. Still, it was a case. Gandhi worked hard on it.

He worried about the case going to court. He still felt very shy about talking in front of groups. Gandhi prepared long notes. He would only have to stand up and read them.

The court date came. Gandhi got there very early. He listened as the other lawyer questioned the first witness. Then it was his turn. He stood up and faced the court. Everyone waited.

Gandhi smiled and nodded. Even the witness wondered what was going on. He smiled back. The young lawyer opened his mouth. No words would come out. He looked at his notes. They were clear. He would just read them. But he just couldn't speak.

The court room began to swim before his eyes. Gandhi thought he might black out. He had to get out of there. People began whispering. Their whispers sounded like a roar in Gandhi's ears.

He turned and looked about the room. There! There was another lawyer. He rushed to him.

"Take over for me," Gandhi said to him. Then he walked quickly out of the court room.

That did it. Gandhi would not get any more cases in the city of Bombay. He did find little jobs—like writing up notes for other lawyers. But no one was about to give him a case to try on his own.

Then a strange thing happened. Gandhi was asked to go to South Africa. Two brothers who lived there owned a big company together. They had gotten into a fight about how to run their company. Both sides had taken lawyers.

One of the lawyers asked Gandhi to come from India to work on the case. Why they asked him, no one is quite sure. They said they could pay for his trip to South Africa. After that, there would be very little pay.

Gandhi saw no other way out. He was failing in India. Maybe in South Africa he would finally do something right. He left his family behind. (He now had two sons.) And he sailed for South Africa.

South Africa, like India, was ruled by Great Britain. Gandhi was used to seeing the English push others around. But the truth of this was thrown in his face in South Africa.

After getting off the ship, Gandhi had to ride a train to Pretoria. In that city he would meet the people he'd be working with.

Gandhi had booked himself a first class seat. He had a long train ride ahead of him. So he sat back and got comfortable. He would catch some sleep. Suddenly he felt someone poke him. He jumped awake.

"Get out!" a man roared.

"What?"

"I said get back to the third class car."

"There's been a mistake," Gandhi said looking straight at the man. "Let me show you my first class ticket."

"Police!" the man called. One showed up right away. He looked first at the white man and then at Gandhi. By the light in his eye Gandhi saw he would not be a friend.

"You have to ride in the back," the policeman said. "In the third class car with the rest of the colored people."

"But I tell you, I have—"

"Makes no difference. Move quickly—or I'll kick you off the train."

Gandhi sat there for a minute. He had always been shy. He had never liked to make waves. But he had grown a lot in the past few years. He was outgrowing his shyness. New, stronger feelings were taking its place. For one, feelings of what was fair and just.

Gandhi looked the policeman in the eye. He sat back in his seat and picked up his newspaper. He refused to move.

The two white men couldn't believe their eyes. Who was this upstart! In South Africa, Indian and black men did as they said.

The train slid into the next stop. The policeman had gone to get help. He came back with two more policemen. First they threw Gandhi's bags off the train. Then, three big men, each two times his size, threw Gandhi off. Then the train took off. It left Gandhi in a strange town in the middle of a country he didn't know.

Gandhi didn't move for a long time. He just sat on the hard ground where he had been thrown. His bags lay around, some broken open. Night had begun to fall. It also began to get very cold. Still Gandhi sat without moving for several hours, lost in thought.

When he finally stood up, Gandhi knew his life had been changed. This was a turning point. He had only been in South Africa for two days. But in that time he had seen enough. As in India, South Africa had only a very small number of white people. Most of the people in the country were black or Indian. Yet these few white people were the rulers. And they acted towards others as if they were dogs.

The next day was the same story all over again. Gandhi was to ride in a coach for the last leg of his trip. He was about to climb in it. But a man said his ticket was not "in order." Gandhi pushed the question. They finally explained. An Indian man could not ride in the same coach as a white man.

Gandhi argued. At last they said he could ride on the outside of the coach. He didn't want to give in to this. But he had to get to Pretoria by the end of the day. So Gandhi climbed onto an outside seat. He held on tight and the coach bumped along.

Meanwhile, a white man decided he wanted to have a smoke. That meant he wanted to sit on the outside seat—where Gandhi was riding.

Well, he wasn't going to sit next to an Indian man. So he tried to order Gandhi off the coach. Gandhi would not move.

"Okay," the man snapped. "You can sit at my feet."

Once again, Gandhi refused to move. The

white man's face turned very red. Gandhi sat still on the seat looking straight ahead. All of a sudden, he felt a sharp pain in his leg. Then another. And another. The man, much bigger than Gandhi, was kicking him as hard as he could.

"What's going on—" A woman put her head out the coach window. "Are you out of your mind?" she asked the man. "Do let the Indian man come sit with us while you smoke."

"Thank you." Gandhi nodded to the woman and climbed in the coach. Living and working in South Africa was not going to be easy.

6

A Trouble-Maker in South Africa

Little did Gandhi know he was going to spend 20 years of his life in South Africa. But it was there he began doing things right at last. The law case he had come to work on was a hard one. He had to do a lot of reading. But in the end, he did very well. In fact, he worked it out so that both sides were happier.

The case took a long time. When it was finished, he had begun other important work. His night sitting in that train station had changed Gandhi for good. He had done a lot of thinking.

He had also seen much, much more in the following months. In some parts of the country, Indians could not vote. They could not own land. And they could not go out after 9:00 at night without a pass. They could never use the sidewalk—they were supposed to walk in the street.

The British were trying to tighten the rules for Indians in South Africa. They wanted to make Indians carry ID cards at all times. This was called the Pass Law or Black Act.

Gandhi decided to stay in South Africa and fight his people's cause. He had been to school and was a lawyer. He saw it as his job to work for his people.

Gandhi called a meeting for Indians. He stood up before the big group. He felt light-headed for a minute. He had not forgotten the time in court when he couldn't speak. But this time he had something too important to say to be shy.

"I have called our people together today—" Gandhi began. He told them of the new laws. He told them they would fight back—as one group. "But we will fight without violence. We will be proud—but we will not be foolish. We will *not* go with their rules. And we will go to jail if it comes to that."

"Kill the British!" one man sang out in the middle of Gandhi's talk.

Gandhi closed his eyes for a moment. "No," he said quietly. "We will kill no one. Not one man in this room—not one Indian in South Africa—will lift a finger against the British. Our cause is right, and that is enough to win."

Gandhi was still young. But he was discovering his power. The people at this meeting were getting a first taste of Gandhi's magic. It was a magic he would work for the next 50 years—the power to move great groups of people.

"Who here will stand with me?" Gandhi called out to the room of men. "Who here will stand with me against this new Pass Law?"

The room was deadly silent. Only the intake of deep breaths could be heard. Then one man stood up. The man next to him stood, also. Then another and another. Gandhi waited. A small smile played at the corners of his mouth. Within seconds the whole room of men stood at Gandhi's word. Gandhi stepped down, knowing that they would stand by him to the end.

Next he had to go home to India and get his family. He missed Kasturbai and his sons. And it looked like he might be in South Africa for a long time. He left for India.

A few weeks later, a ship sailed back with Gandhi and his family aboard. Gandhi felt happy and strong. He was fired up for the work ahead of him. When the ship landed, a man was waiting for Gandhi. He climbed on board to talk with him.

"Mr. Gandhi," he said. "You must stay on the ship until dark. The people have heard of your talks here in South Africa. They say you have been spreading lies in India about our ways. You must wait until the mob out there breaks up. Then you can get off the ship."

"Oh, don't be silly." Gandhi waved the man away. "I have nothing to hide. I will leave the ship in the light of day."

"Well, yes, of course you shouldn't have to hide anything. But I don't believe it's safe out there for you and your family. Take a ride, at least."

"My family will ride," Gandhi said. "And I

will walk. We don't need to talk of this anymore."

They got off the boat. Gandhi helped Kasturbai and his sons into a coach. He set out on foot behind them, talking with a friend.

In the next moment Gandhi did not see his friend. People were pushing in closely. Then he realized what was happening. A group of white boys had circled him. They had cut him off from his friend. Next thing he knew, a rock hit his head. Someone kicked him hard. Gandhi fell to the ground. And the boys fell on top of him.

Completely by luck, the chief of police's wife was passing by just then. She was a brave woman. She threw herself on the group of boys who were beating on Gandhi. They backed off when they saw a woman was in their circle. Then they saw who she was and took off at a run.

Someone helped Gandhi up. The woman called her husband. The chief of police himself came to help. He took Gandhi to the house where he and his family were staying.

The danger was not over, however. An even

bigger mob came together outside the gate of the house. They had discovered where Gandhi was staying.

These people were not happy with Gandhi's ideas. They saw him as a dangerous man. Dangerous, that is, to their way of life. They wanted to let him know he was not going to get away with it.

Rocks crashed through the windows. People shouted from the street, "Hang Gandhi! Hang Gandhi!"

Once again the chief of police stepped in. He sent two policemen to help Gandhi get out of the house. They dressed him in other people's clothing. That way people wouldn't know who he was—unless they got a good look. The police made sure no one got a good look. They slid out the back door with Gandhi.

The three men jumped the back fence. They ran down back streets. They kept clear of street lights. And finally, they made it safely to the police station.

After that, people in South Africa left Gandhi and his family alone. He set up a law practice. And he did very well. He also continued to work for the rights of Indians.

One day there was a great pounding on his door. He stood up as a man just about fell into his law office. Gandhi could see that the man was an untouchable. And that he was hurt. His face was a mess. Some of his teeth had been knocked out. He had two black eyes. The man had been badly beaten.

"What happened to you?" Gandhi rushed to the man and helped him into a chair.

The man had to catch his breath. He looked around, not sure if he should be here. An untouchable in a law office! But this was Mohandas K. Gandhi. His friends had said it was okay. Still, the man felt out of place.

"My master has beat me—again," the man said. His eyes were looking this way and that but never at Gandhi. "My friends have told me of your kindness. They told me you sometimes find it in your heart to help a poor untouchable like me. Because you are so very, very kind—"

"Cut the pretty words," Gandhi snapped. "I am wearing this suit and tie. And you are in rags. But that does not mean you have to bow before me. Stand up. Of course, I will do what I can."

The next week Gandhi was able to find the man a kinder master. Word spread like fire among the Indians in South Africa. A man of Gandhi's caste helped an untouchable. This had never been done before. More and more Indians of all castes turned to Gandhi for help.

In Gandhi's own mind, the whole thing had hardly been made better. He found the man a kinder master, it was true. But why must any man be master of another, kind or not?

Gandhi spent more and more time on the cause of the untouchables. He fought against such ideas as: *A Hindu of higher caste can't drink from the same well as an untouchable. The shadow of an untouchable cannot pass over a Hindu of a higher caste. Untouchables must do all the dirty work.*

Gandhi put his words into practice, too. He began doing things like washing his own clothes. He didn't always do it very well. Other lawyers laughed at the way his home-washed suits looked in court.

"You look as if you have rats in your hair!" a lawyer told him one day laughing.

"I cut my own hair today," Gandhi explained, "because a white hair cutter refused to touch an Indian's head."

Gandhi had a thicker skin these days. He had learned to laugh a lot more. "Well," he said to these lawyers. "I can save money on my washing and make you laugh at the same time. I guess we're all happier this way."

Gandhi was taking a different stand on Indian rights now. Before he had fought for the right to ride first class in trains. Now he would only ride third class. He said all people were equal. Untouchables could not ride with him in first class. So he would ride with them in third. He called the untouchables an Indian word that meant "children of God."

Gandhi continued reading about all religions. He believed they were all right and good. He believed Christians, Muslims, Hindus and Jews should live together peacefully.

Gandhi also read and learned about giving birth to babies. He was the "doctor" for Kasturbai's next two children.

Not everyone in South Africa liked Gandhi's different ideas. Kasturbai, a strong Hindu, had the hardest time of all. He wanted her to live as he did. As usual, she fought him tooth and nail the whole way.

Besides washing his own clothes, Gandhi did other "untouchable work." He believed, for one, that everyone should take a turn cleaning the bathroom.

This Kasturbai would not do. It was against her religion. She believed God would turn against her if she did. Another one of their big fights broke out.

"I refuse!" she screamed.

"If you were such a good Hindu woman, you would not have such a strong will," Gandhi yelled back at her. "And you would do as your husband said!"

Kasturbai fiercely grabbed the cleaning things. She saw that her husband would have his way. But Gandhi took hold of her arm.

"Let go of me! What are you doing? Can't you see I am going to clean?"

"But you must do it with a smile. I will not stand for the way you are acting in my house."

"Then keep your house to yourself," Kasturbai

fired back. "And let me go."

Still holding her arm, Gandhi started pulling her to the door. He was so mad he completely lost his head. Kasturbai tripped and fell, but he didn't stop. He dragged her to the front gate.

"What are you doing?" she cried through her tears. "Where can I go? I have no family here to take me in. Do you think you can act this way toward me just because I am your wife? Please stop and close the gate. What do you think the neighbors will think of you?"

Gandhi did let go of her then. Suddenly he was filled with shame. He didn't understand Kasturbai. But he realized he had no right to act as her master. He said he was sorry, and they made up.

7

The Beginning of *Soul Force*

In 1906 the Black Act was passed in South Africa. That was the law Gandhi had stayed in the country to fight. The Black Act said that all Indians had to carry ID cards. Of course, white people didn't have to carry anything.

"Don't worry," Gandhi told his people. By now the Indians of South Africa looked to him as their leader. "We have said we will stand together as a group. We have said we will not live with this law. And we know the British cannot jail 20,000 Indians."

The man behind this law was named General Smuts. He was head of the Transvaal government (a part of South Africa). He was also head of the British army there. Gandhi went to speak to him.

"I've come to tell you I'm going to fight the Black Act," he told Smuts.

Smuts laughed in his face. People had told him to watch out for this Mohandas K. Gandhi man. But he had to laugh now that he saw him. Why had anyone worried about what this little Indian would do? Ha! So he wanted to take on the British government, did he?

"Is that all you want to tell me?" Smuts asked with a smile. How could the man be so foolish. He was telling his enemy what he was going to do. "Anything else you want to say?"

"Yes," said Gandhi. "Not only am I going to fight the Black Act. I am also going to win."

"Oh?" So the little man wants to get smart with me, thought Smuts. "How do you plan to do that?"

Now it was Gandhi's turn to smile. He answered, "With your help."

Smuts got angry now. He called for a man to show Gandhi out. Going out the door, Gandhi turned and said, "Thank you." He believed in acting toward your enemy as you would toward a friend.

Next Gandhi rounded up the Indian people. He spoke to them as he had before.

"We will not sign up for our ID cards. We will not give into the Black Act. *Not one of us.*" The people at the meeting yelled and clapped for Gandhi. He held up a hand to quiet them. "Not only that, we will have no fear. For fear leads to hate. They may try to strike us. They may throw us in jail. But we will not hit back. We will fill the jails. But we will not give in!"

In the next few weeks thousands and thousands of Indians refused to sign up for ID cards. Gandhi went to jail along with these thousands. The whole thing quickly got out of hand. The jails were running out of space. It took a lot of money to feed that many people. Something had to be done. Gandhi's plan was working.

"Tell Gandhi I want to see him," General Smuts ordered. His man in waiting went to get Gandhi. When Gandhi stood before him, he said, "Look, Gandhi, so you've pulled a good one on me. OK, I'll take back the Black Act. And I'll let you and your friends out of jail. But only if all of the Indians sign up for the cards first. Sign up, and then I'll take back the Black Act."

Gandhi eyed Smuts. Why would they have to sign up if he was only going to drop the law afterwards? Probably to save face, Gandhi guessed. Then Smuts would look like he won. And when he later took back the law, he would look like a good guy.

"Okay," Gandhi said. "I'll tell the people." Smuts shot out his hand. Gandhi took it, and they shook hands as two men on equal ground.

Many people were fiercely angry at Gandhi. Some turned their backs on their leader. How could Gandhi have said yes to this? Did he really want them to sign up? Thousands had gone to jail for *not* signing up.

What happened next made people even madder. Most of the Indian people signed up. They got their ID cards. And then General Smuts left the Black Act just as it was.

Gandhi had been ready to believe Smuts. Still, he was not surprised that Smuts had tricked him. The man had not been good to his word. Gandhi was ready to make his next move.

He and his followers built a huge fire. One by one they would drop the ID cards onto the fire.

Gandhi went first. The police were standing by. They waited on horseback. Each one had a heavy stick in his hand. Kasturbai and other women stood close by also. Gandhi believed women must come out of their houses. He believed they must help fight for Indian rights. Kasturbai had begun helping. She had gotten a group of women together for the ID card burning.

As Gandhi got closer to the fire, the police circled in. Gandhi reached his hand out holding his ID card. He was about to drop it on the fire. A police stick cracked down on his hand. He dropped the pass into the fire anyway.

Then he went and took the passes from his friends. He walked back to the fire with them. The police closed in again. Kasturbai's hands flew to her mouth. She cried out for Mohandas to stop. The other women held her back when she tried to run to him.

The police beat Gandhi badly. He was kicked and hit over the head with sticks. When the police left at last, Gandhi lay in a pile in the mud. But every ID card had burned in the fire.

That night Kasturbai held ice to his head. She cleaned the cuts.

"Why must you be this way?" she asked him. "So stubborn."

"I'd die before I'd live with such laws. Don't you understand, Kasturbai?"

"Of course you are right. But to get beaten so badly—what good does that do?"

Gandhi bowed his head. "I am learning about a new kind of power," he said in a soft voice. "I have read a lot about it in Hindu teachings. It is called *soul force*. It is the power of love and truth mixed up together. It is a way to change people's hearts—not just their laws."

"If you keep this up, you will soon be dead," replied Kasturbai. "Then you will change nothing."

"They can beat me all they want. I am used to it now. But soon they will learn. The power of *soul force* is catching."

Kasturbai just shook her head at her husband. He was so stubborn. She believed in him. But sometimes she thought he didn't realize what hardships he put on his family. He wanted to live that way. And so they must all.

"Kasturbai," Gandhi said even more softly. "Don't you know I've learned so much of this from you? The times I have tried to make your will my own. The times I've tried to force you to think and do as I say. Those times I was wrong, very wrong. Yet you did not give into my wrong-doing. Talk about stubborn!" Gandhi laughed. Then he was thoughtful again.

"No, you stuck to what you believed. And in your love for me—well, you changed me. For you see, my putting my ideas on you was a kind of violence, too. *Soul force* is more than believing. It is doing. Doing what is right and in no way taking part in what is wrong. When you would not give in to me, that's what you were doing.

"So you see," Gandhi went on. "I am only practicing what I learned from you. So you must go along with me."

"What?" Kasturbai stood back. "That's very

tricky, Mohandas. See, you are trying once again to bend my will. But you thought you could trick me by using the back door!"

Gandhi threw back his head and laughed. The joke was on him and he knew it. Yes, he had been trying to bend her will once again.

"You are always right, my dear Kasturbai."

"Ha!" she snorted. "You can talk circles around me because you have read so many books. But I know what I believe."

Thousands of other Indians did as Gandhi and his friends did. All over South Africa they burned their ID cards. Once again Smuts threw people in jail. The jails were soon overflowing.

Smuts was lost for what to do. There was no more room in the jails. And this upstart Gandhi was making matters worse every day. He had made Indians feel it was *good* to go to jail.

Besides the overflowing jails, there were other problems. Indians filled many of the lowest paying jobs in South African companies. They made up a big part of the work force. With all the Indians in jail, many companies were having to shut down. Of course, this was Gandhi's idea.

At last Smuts gave in. He had no other way out. He took back the Black Act. And he set the jailed Indians free.

General Smuts was a tricky man. And there isn't too much good to say about him. But here's one thing: when he knew he had lost, he said so. And to the day he died, he spoke highly of Gandhi. "There was a man," he said, "who no one could hate. Gandhi is a better man than any of us will ever be."

As for Gandhi, he thought it was time to go home. He had been in South Africa for 20 years. He had thought he was going for only a few months. Now he was 45 years old. And he longed to see the shores of India again.

Gandhi had never wanted to take part in politics. He had other ideas for what to do with the rest of his life. He and his family packed their bags and boarded a ship for India.

8

Life on the Ashram in India

Gandhi stood at the front of the ship. He put his neck out and looked hard. There it was, the shore of India.

The ship sailed quickly. Gandhi remembered the last time he had gotten off a ship. He had been returning to South Africa. The group of boys had tried to beat him up.

The Indian leader was used to danger by now. He had many enemies. People who didn't want Indians to have equal rights with white people in South Africa. He wondered what the

British rulers in India thought of him. He hoped he and his family would land safely on home shores.

As he stepped off the boat, however, a group closed in on him. He felt people grab hold of him. Gandhi jumped back on the walkway that ran from the ship to shore. He held Kasturbai and the children back.

"Stand back!" Gandhi ordered.

"But look," said Kasturbai. "They are all Indians." It was true. Gandhi looked out at a sea of white clothing. The faces of thousands of Indians were turned toward him. And they were all calling out, "Mahatma Gandhi! Mahatma Gandhi!" These were friends, not enemies.

Gandhi's face turned very red. They were calling him "mahatma." That meant "great soul." Gandhi did not think of himself as great at all. It made him feel silly when people talked that way. He brushed a hand through the air at them. As if you could brush away thousands of people!

Little had he known Indians in India had been following his every move. They knew all about his work in South Africa. And they were very glad to take him as their leader here.

Pushing through the people was not easy. Everyone wanted to see the Mahatma. Gandhi was very glad when they arrived at last at the home of friends.

In his first few weeks he had many visitors. A movement had begun in India. A group of men were fighting for home rule. That meant they wanted Indians to rule India, not the British.

These important men came to Gandhi asking for his help. They had heard of his power to move giant groups of people. They knew of the love Indians had for him. If Gandhi would join them, they were sure to win home rule soon.

Gandhi told them no. He was through with politics. He had other plans. Gandhi left these important men in the big cities. And he went to the heart of India. There he set up his ashram.

An ashram is a group of people living and working together. On Gandhi's ashram everyone did all kinds of work. People from all castes and religions could live there. Christians, Jews and Hindus lived there. A family of untouchables moved there later. No one on Gandhi's ashram was any more or less important than anyone else. By now even Kasturbai was used to cleaning the bathrooms.

It was fiercely hot in the middle of India. But Gandhi worked hard. He was always having new ideas—about food, clothing, people, everything. He often decided what they would eat at the ashram. And the meals could be very strange. No meat, of course.

Then he started having a day of silence once a week. On that day he would only pray and work quietly. (Sometimes he did cheat, though. He would write notes to people.)

Gandhi traveled a great deal. He traveled by foot, walking from one small village to the next. He walked for days. He was getting money for the poor, mostly for the untouchables (or "children of God" as he called them). This was the kind of life he loved best.

Very few Indians were rich. But if they had any money, the men bought gold for their wives. Women wore gold to show the family's station in life. Or to show how rich they were.

One day a woman was doing the washing in front of her home. She lived in a small village.

The day was hot. And the sun was shining brightly. Gold hung from her ears and around her neck. It flashed in the sunlight. She was very proud of it. She and her husband had worked hard for it.

As she worked her clothes over a washboard, she heard some children shouting. A group of them were running in the road. Behind them the woman saw a strange looking fellow. He was very skinny and had great ears. His head was shaved. He wore funny little round glasses. And he wore only one cloth tied on like a pair of shorts. The man had a walking stick about as big as his leg. And it was much taller than himself. Small as he was, he moved toward her at a breakneck speed.

The man stopped before her and smiled. The children still danced around him. They seemed to love him and she could see why. His eyes shined. And he cracked one joke after another. When the children laughed, so did he. He threw back his head and opened his mouth. She saw he had very few teeth left.

"Good morning," he said to her at last. "My name is Mohandas K. Gandhi."

"Oh, my!" the woman cried. She had heard

of this man. She began to call her husband. But Gandhi held up his hand and said not to bother him. He simply wanted to ask about her gold.

"My gold?" she asked. What was he getting at?

"Yes," Gandhi said. "What I am about to say is quite bold. But thousands of Indians have nothing to eat. Maybe you would like to give your gold. My friends and I would sell it and buy food for the hungry. India is so full of poor people, you know."

The woman looked at him like he was a madman for a second. One of the older boys seemed to be her son. He whispered in her ear, "I'll go get Daddy. Don't give him a thing."

"No," the woman said holding her son back. She still hadn't taken her eyes off Gandhi. "No, it's okay."

The woman let go of her son's arm. She reached up and took off the gold pieces. Her son's eyes were very big as she handed the gold to Gandhi.

"May God bless you," Gandhi said with a little bow. He put the gold in a little bag he carried. Then he began to play with the children again. They took off down the street.

Word spread of Gandhi's travels. Everyone in India learned what he was doing. After a while, folks ran out in the road when they saw him coming into a village. The women pushed and shoved to be the first to give Gandhi their gold. People began to say he worked a very special magic.

But not everyone thought he was so wonderful. The British rulers, for one. They watched Gandhi closely. But they weren't too worried about him. What could this skinny man do to the British Empire? So he walked from village to village helping the poor. What of it?

A few British leaders said maybe they had better keep an eye on him. They remembered what he had done in South Africa. But others laughed this off. Maybe as an up-and-coming young Indian lawyer in South Africa he had some power. But look at the man now! Gandhi was getting more and more strange by the day.

Gandhi had quit wearing suits and ties. Now he wore only white cloth made in India. Usually he wore just one piece. If it was cold, he put another around his shoulders.

Then there were his funny looks. And his funny food. His day of silence. His 5 to 20 mile walks every day (even when he wasn't traveling). He took to fasting, too. A fast is going without food. He would fast for days sometimes. It was his way of making up for a wrong-doing. He would fast for his own wrong-doing or for someone else's.

To top it off, the man lived in the middle of a giant country. He couldn't be a danger to anyone out there. Or so they thought.

Then Gandhi started his spinning. The cotton mills in England sold much of their cloth to India. Clothing 400,000,000 people takes a lot of cloth. And the English made them pay dearly for it.

Gandhi said Indians should make their own cotton. That way they wouldn't have to pay so much for it. And they would show the English that they didn't need them.

As usual, the English laughed at Gandhi's idea. There was this funny looking 45-year-old man spinning cotton on a spinning wheel.

But as he went from town to village, he told people to spin. He called the cotton homespun.

Gandhi at his spinning wheel. (Wide World)

He himself spun 200 yards of homespun a day. (Kasturbai had to teach him how. She thought he was very funny at first. She hadn't forgotten the times he had tried to teach her to read. Now she could get back at him.)

Believe it or not, the idea caught on. Indians all over began spinning their own cotton. They stopped buying clothes made in England. Cotton mills in England had to close down. The English lost a great deal of money.

"This," Gandhi told the people, "is *soul force* at its best. We will not give in to being sat upon. We will fight back with our own hard work."

9

Nehru and the Revolutionaries

Some Indian leaders for home rule didn't like Gandhi's ideas. All their lives they had tried to get the respect that white men get. Then here was Gandhi riding third class in trains! And there he was giving up fine English suits for homespun. What kind of respect would that win?

"You let them treat you like a dog when you dress in those funny clothes," they would say.

"These are Indian clothes."

"Yes, but—"

"Yes, but what?" Gandhi shot back. "Because the British wear suits does that make them better? I should think not. If you want respect as an Indian, you must act like one. Don't try to be an Englishman. You will never get the skin color right."

Gandhi threw back his head and gave out his horse-like laugh. The other Indian leaders rolled their eyes. They were forever saying, "But Gandhi!" Then they would ask questions. A few of them were listening—and learning.

"Well, then, what about the untouchables. Can we really let them be a part of our—"

"You want equal rights with white men. But you don't want to give equal rights to your own Indian brothers. No Indians will be free until we *all* are free."

"But Gandhi, why do you have to travel third class?"

"Because there is no fourth class."

The revolutionary might look at his hands and then up again. "Listen, I know you are right. You are right about the untouchables. But we must be real. First independence. Then we'll talk about equal rights."

"No," said Gandhi. "Indians will not be free until every man and woman in India is free."

By the fire in his eye, they would see Gandhi had had enough. He was known to up and leave a room in the middle of a meeting. "Gandhi! Where are you going?" someone would call. Maybe they had flown in that morning just to talk to him.

"To feed the goats," Gandhi would answer. He would not come back for several hours.

Still these revolutionaries came to see Gandhi wherever he was. Being in the heart of the country didn't stop these men. They flew. They walked. They did whatever they had to do to talk to Gandhi. For Gandhi held the key to the Indian people. There would be no revolution without him. The Indian leaders knew this. They would have to put up with his strange ways.

One day a young Indian revolutionary came to visit Gandhi at his ashram. His name was Nehru. Nehru had been raised in a well-to-do Hindu family. And he had gone to the best British schools. He had become one of the most important leaders for home rule.

Nehru had heard of Gandhi's nonviolence

and *soul force*. But he believed those ways for change would take too long. He wanted Indian independence. And he wanted it now. He thought he could talk Gandhi into joining his revolutionary friends.

Nehru arrived at the ashram one evening. He asked to see Gandhi. Gandhi said he would be very happy to talk with him. Why doesn't Nehru join him on his morning walk?

The walk began at 5:00 the next morning. Nehru was surprised to see others were joining them. There was quite a group.

Gandhi shot out like he was in a big hurry. Some children ran alongside of him. Nehru had thought he was in good shape. He had always done well in sports. But he was having to trot to keep up with this skinny old man.

"Mr. Gandhi?" Nehru tried to get a place beside Gandhi. They had important things to talk about and he wanted to get started. "Uh, Mr. Gandhi?"

Gandhi, however, was in the middle of telling a joke. Nehru was not able to get close to him. There were too many children pushing around the man.

Finally the children fell away. Nehru was out of breath by now. He had to keep taking big skipping steps to keep up. This made him angry. Nehru was an important man.

"Mr. Gandhi, please?" He tried again. But now Gandhi was talking with one of his helpers. Finally Gandhi turned to Nehru.

"Mr. Nehru?"

They had gone several miles now. Nehru wanted to ask if they might slow down a little. He didn't think he could run and talk about Indian independence at the same time.

"Gandhi," Nehru gasped.

Gandhi turned and saw the man's red face. His English suit was wet through. Nehru didn't need to say a word. Gandhi decided to cut his walk short this morning. They turned around. And over breakfast, Nehru finally got to have his say.

Nehru told Gandhi about the revolution he wanted. He told Gandhi how important it was that it happened now.

Gandhi heard him out. He let Nehru talk for a long time. Then he said his piece.

"You people are always talking about revolution," Gandhi told him. "Well, I am making one. What's revolutionary about violence? Do you really love the Indian people, your own people? Then help me show them how to turn their backs on violence. Help me show them how to throw off fear. Do you really believe we can stop English violence with Indian violence? No. We will win independence. And we will do it with love in our hearts."

Nehru left the ashram believing Gandhi. This was the beginning of a lifelong friendship.

Nehru even gave up his English suits. He said he would not be comfortable going around in one piece of homespun (like Gandhi). But he began wearing Indian clothes. And he began to work for independence Gandhi's way—without violence.

Gandhi could not hide from politics. The people were finding him at his ashram. Letters and telegrams poured in every day. In fact, so many that they had to put in a special post office out at the ashram. Then they had to put in a telegraph office, too. Like it or not, Gandhi belonged to the people.

10

India Goes Out on Strike

In 1914 World War One broke out. Most of the fighting was done in Europe. But since England ruled India, that country was pulled into the war also.

Surprisingly, Gandhi helped the British. He took care of people who had been hurt. He did this because England had as much as promised independence to India—if they helped fight the war.

Gandhi's followers were tired of him always falling for these promises. Didn't he ever

Nehru talks with Gandhi, 1946. (UPI/Bettmann)

learn? In some ways, the man was like a child. He was willing to believe anyone. He thought everyone had a good heart. Some people were just out of touch with theirs.

Sure enough, the war ended and not a word was said about Indian independence. In fact, new laws were passed. These laws tightened the British hold on India. Thousands and thousands of Indians were mad. And so was Gandhi.

After World War One, the United States was the big power in the world. The American president called on England to give India its independence. Britain, however, still refused to let go of its most prized holding.

His new friend Nehru and some other Indian leaders called Gandhi to a meeting. They were ready to take up arms. The time had come to fight.

"No," said Gandhi.

The other men looked at him. One said, "Listen, Gandhi. Your way of *soul force* has done much for India. We have shown Britain some of our strength. But that is old now. It is time to fight—really fight. How much longer can we play your games with a spinning wheel?"

Gandhi lifted his bowed head. He looked tired. "We will not use one gun. We will not cause any blood—"

"Are the rest of you going to listen to this silly—" The man tried to cut Gandhi off. But Nehru stepped in. Nehru did not want to wait forever for independence, either. And sometimes Gandhi's strange ways made him really angry. They had many political differences. Still, Nehru believed in Gandhi. And he knew his power. "Let Gandhi speak," Nehru said.

"Here is what we're going to do," Gandhi said. "On the day we say, the whole country of India will go on strike. Every man, woman and child will stop working. That will close down every company. We will stop the mail. We will stop every train from running. And the country of India will have a day of prayer and fasting."

Two of the men met eyes over Gandhi's head. They shook their heads. "Oh, please Gandhi. Be for real. How could we ever get everyone in one of the biggest countries in the world to stop work? How can we tell everyone about it? The idea is foolish."

"We will do it," said Gandhi. "And it will work."

Nehru wasn't sure, but he was willing to give it a try. The other men just let out long sighs. They knew Gandhi would have his way.

As usual, Gandhi wrote to the British rulers in India. He told them about the strike. And he told them why he was doing it. They laughed as they read the note from Gandhi.

"The Indians in South Africa were one thing," they said. "But maybe he doesn't realize how big India is. What a joke."

"Should we throw him in jail?" another British leader asked.

"Throw him in jail? What for? There's no way under the sun he can pull this off. Don't lose any sleep over it." The men laughed and threw the letter away.

Maybe this time Gandhi had taken on more than he could handle. His friends thought he was dreaming. But they set to work anyway.

By now Gandhi had many followers carrying on his work. They were spread out across the country. They rode the trains from town to town just as Gandhi did. And they stayed in touch with the Mahatma.

Gandhi set the day. And he sent out the word. As always, he clearly warned the people that there would be no violence.

On the morning of the strike, April 16, 1919, the sun rose over a silent India. Thousands of Indians ran out in the streets to listen to the silence. Ships sat still close to shore. Trains didn't move an inch. Shops were closed. Not a wheel turned in India.

Britain's most prized country—the one that made it the most money—had ground to a standstill. And the British could not jail 400,000,000 Indians. They couldn't do a thing.

Gandhi was well pleased. The British would lose a lot of money. But even more, they would see that Indians could stand together as one group. They did not need Britain. Best of all, the people were standing together *in peace*. Gandhi thought that maybe the people had truly been trained in the powers of *soul force*.

But he was wrong. A few had decided to take matters into their own hands. A fight broke out in the town of Amritsan. And three English people were killed.

Gandhi was very sad. You might think that a small handful of violent men is nothing. After all, India is a country of 400,000,000 people. Think how many were peacefully striking. But even one act of violence made Gandhi unhappy.

A man named General Dyer ran the British army in Amritsan. He wanted to get back at the Indians for the three men killed. He wasn't going to sit around and see the British get stepped upon. He would teach these Indians.

In the middle of Amritsan was a big walled-in square. There the peaceful people of the town were meeting. A man stood on a box and was speaking to the group of 10,000. He was a teacher of Gandhi's way of nonviolence.

Meanwhile General Dyer got together a small group of armed men. Leading the men, General Dyer marched toward the square. When the Indian people were in sight, the army stopped. The general began barking out orders.

Fifteen men all fell to one knee. They were in

a line facing the 10,000 people.

"General Dyer, please?" one man in his army asked.

The general turned his head to hear what the man had to say.

"Don't you think we should give them a warning? Give them a chance to leave?"

"They've had their chance," Dyer growled.

Some of the Indian people had seen the army by now. They didn't know what was going to happen, but it wasn't going to be good. The whole square was walled-in. There were only one or two doors out.

"Lift your guns!" he ordered. "Ready! . . . Set! . . . Fire!"

The fifteen men opened fire on the group. Men, women and children alike fell with each shot that rang out. Babies screamed. Mothers looked wildly about for their children. People ran for the two doors out.

After ten minutes, 150 people had been shot dead. Others had died by jumping in a well to get out of the line of fire. Over 1,500 were badly hurt. General Dyer and his men fired

1,650 shots—and they hit their mark 1,516 times.

Then the general left the square. And he did not send help to the 1,500 who were hurt but not dead.

Gandhi was broken-hearted. He believed he was the cause of this violence. He had called for the country-wide strike. If he hadn't done so, this would not have happened.

At the same time he was angry, really angry. Gandhi had always believed the British were *trying* to do the right thing—until now. Gandhi's friends were glad to see his eyes opened at last. When it came to India, the British had done nothing right. They wanted only the money they could wring out of the poor country.

Gandhi wrote another letter to the British head of India. He wrote: "I have given you all the chances I can. It is time for all out war between your people and mine. Only we will fight my kind of war. And that is war without violence. We will force you out of India peacefully with love and truth."

Gandhi called for noncooperation. Noncooperation meant not helping the British in any way. Gandhi said:

Do not use the British courts of law.
Give up jobs with British companies.
Leave your government jobs.
Do not buy anything made in Britain.
Try to pay no taxes.

This time the British took note. By now they knew the power of Gandhi's *soul force*. Still they were lost for what to do. This was certainly a new kind of revolution. You can't jail someone for leaving a job. How can you force someone to buy cloth made in Britain?

Noncooperation was working, too. Gandhi took to the road again. In every town he told the people what they should do. He built giant fires. The people threw their British-made clothes on the fire. Gandhi talked them into wearing only homespun.

People left their jobs everywhere. Policemen, postmen, workers in companies. Without the workers, the British government had little to stand on. British companies slowed to a crawl.

Gandhi had proved himself a big danger to the British at last. They had to put a stop to this.

They began throwing people in jail. Soon 50,000 Indians were in jail.

Gandhi was left free. Some say that was because the British were worried about violence. They knew only Gandhi could keep the peace. The noncooperation went on for two years. And in that time there had not been one outbreak of violence. If they jailed Gandhi, the whole country might break into war.

Then it happened. Some British police fired on a group of Indians. This group of Indians couldn't take it any more. They turned on the police. They chased them back inside the city hall. Then they set the hall on fire. Some police died inside. Others got beaten as they ran out of the burning building.

Gandhi called off the strike of non-cooperation. He was deeply sorry for what had happened. The people were not ready for a nonviolent revolution, he said. Then he went on a five-day fast to make up for the violence.

"What!" people cried. "Give up the strike? But it's working beautifully!" The British were at their breaking point. They would have had to give in any day soon. Independence was around the corner.

"No," Gandhi said. "I don't care how close Indian independence is. Independence by means of violence isn't worth a thing."

"But Gandhi," Nehru tried to talk to the stubborn man. "One outbreak of Indian violence in two years! Do you know how many times British police have killed and beaten Indians? In two years time our people have fought back just this once. Can't you see the good side of anything?"

"I will see *only* the good side," Gandhi said. "That is why I'm calling off the strike. I have had to see a bad side of my people. We are not ready for independence until each and every Indian can practice *soul force.*"

Gandhi had never had fewer followers. Many decided he didn't know what he was doing. They were very, very angry with him. It looked as if he'd lost his power over the people at last.

Strangely, this was the time the British decided to throw Gandhi in jail. He had called off the strike. He had lost a large part of his following. Maybe they had just been waiting for their chance.

11

Muslims and Hindus Fight

The Mahatma was always happiest in jail. He had already spent a lot of his life there. This time it was for six years. He loved the quiet time. He could read and pray all he wanted.

Besides, for Gandhi, being in jail was an honor. He made all Indians feel this way. Going to jail for what you believed in was the highest good. Gandhi kicked up his feet for a good six year rest.

But he was only there for a short time when he became very sick. The British were scared.

Gandhi was no longer young. They rushed him to one of their best doctors.

You may wonder why they cared so much. The British were not foolish. If Gandhi died in jail, the people might think he was killed. Then the Indian people might really overturn the British rulers.

Gandhi got well again. Then the British set him free. They had had a scare. They didn't want Gandhi's death on their hands.

Before they let him go they made him sign a letter. The letter said that he had been well taken care of in jail. More and more Gandhi had them where he wanted them. Every step of the way, the British tried to wash their hands of wrong-doing.

Out of jail, Gandhi was disappointed in his people. Great fights had broken out between the Hindus and Muslims. (The Muslims practiced another important religion in India called Islam.) It was practically like a war.

Gandhi began a 21-day fast. And to make his point, he stayed the 21 days in a Muslim home. He let a Christian woman care for him.

"Why?" Gandhi asked anyone who visited

him. "Why can't all God's children live together in peace?"

As the fast went on, no one knew if Gandhi would live. Thousands prayed for him. Thousands traveled to his bedside from miles around. Thousands kneeled beside him. They begged him to end his fast. And they promised to stop fighting.

When he was sure there was peace everywhere, Gandhi ate again. He was ready to go back home.

"No more politics for me," Gandhi said again. He wanted only to help the poor in his country. Leave the talking to others. Gandhi returned to his ashram. He hoped for a quiet life.

However, he could not hold his hands over his ears for long. Indian home rule leaders were once again calling for revolution—a violent revolution right now. "It's time to overthrow the British!" they cried. "And we will do it by force. There are only a handful of them. There are 400,000,000 of us."

"Hold off for one year," Gandhi begged them. "If we are not closer to independence in one year, I will join you."

Meantime, Gandhi kept on spinning his cotton. He kept on teaching the people about *soul force.*

"That's easy for you to say," someone said to him. "You are the Mahatma."

"No," said Gandhi, over and over again. "I do not call myself that. I am not as strong as most people. See?" Gandhi would hold up one of his skinny arms. He would roar with laughter. Then quietly, "Everyone has the power of *soul force.* We have it together."

These days Gandhi got along better with Kasturbai. He knew he had learned a great deal from her. Kasturbai helped Gandhi by working with Indian women.

"Women," Gandhi often said, "know more about *soul force* than anyone. They are more gentle. They have not learned the violent ways of men."

Gandhi's ideas about women had changed a lot over the years. He now saw how equal rights for women would help free men, too. He believed that no real change in India could happen without the help of women. Many of

Gandhi's best workers and leaders were women.

By 1930 no real change had taken place in India. In America, the stock market had crashed the year before. People around the world were feeling the harm. Britain was tightening its hold on India.

Gandhi knew he would have to join in politics again. It was time to act. And he had an idea. Gandhi was going to make salt.

Sound like a strange idea? Well, it was. Here's the thinking behind it. In India salt is the most important thing next to water. The country is very, very hot. And salt helps keep the water in a person. The people in India use lots of salt.

Of course the British knew this. They made it against the law for Indians to make their own salt. Instead, the British made salt and sold it to Indians. They sold it at high prices. The British made a lot of money that way.

Gandhi believed this kind of law was at the very heart of British rule. He was going to break the Salt Law.

Gandhi wrote his usual letter to the British head of India. "Dear Friend," he wrote. He believed that all enemies were just friends who didn't quite understand one another. "I am going to break the law again by making salt. I wanted to let you know first. If there is any way we can work things out differently, I am ready to talk."

As usual, no one answered Gandhi's letter. By now the British didn't laugh at Gandhi. They had learned the hard way how very clever he could be.

"Let's throw him in jail," one said.

"Can't you see it's far too late for that? He has trained thousands and thousands in his way—what do you call it? *Soul force?* If he gives the word, it will happen."

"I suppose you're right. The wheels are already turning. If we throw him in jail, it will only give fire to their cause."

"I say we pretend nothing is happening. We will not give them the time of day."

"Good idea."

The British could pretend all they wanted. But people around the world now knew Mahatma Gandhi. He was in the newspapers of every country. People had begun making movies in the early 1900's. Gandhi was "on the news" everywhere movies were shown. The eyes of the world were on this man.

And the news was making the British look foolish. It was clear to most other countries that India had the right to be free. President Roosevelt in America was asking Britain to give India home rule. But the British held on tight.

"Let Gandhi make salt!" they said. "These Indians can't rule themselves. They have no schooling. They need us to look after them." To the Indians they said, "You people don't know how to rule yourselves."

12

The Salt March

On March 12, 1930, Gandhi set out from his ashram. He had 78 of his friends with him. They were going to walk 240 miles to the sea. There they would make salt.

The Salt March took 24 days. Gandhi stopped in every town along the way to talk to the people. He told them to live cleanly. He told them about the rights of women and untouchables. He told them to give up child marriages. He told them to wear only homespun.

Finally, Gandhi told them why he was marching to the sea. Everyone should wait for him to give the sign. And when he did, they

Mahatma Gandhi and a group of his followers, 1938.
(Wide World)

were all to break the Salt Law. People in Indian sea towns were to make salt. People far from the sea were to buy the unlawful salt. People all over India were ready by the time Gandhi reached the sea.

Gandhi was 61 years old now, but he had never been in better shape. He raced along. He loved to walk fast. People always had trouble keeping up.

In every town people left home and joined Gandhi's Salt March. Others threw flowers at his feet as he passed through. Newspaper writers ran alongside him asking questions. Movie cameras shot him as he pushed ahead. Gandhi reached the sea 24 days later. His group had grown to a few thousand.

He and his followers made camp near the sea. Then Gandhi led prayers. He prayed for no violence on the following day. Most of his friends, however, prayed for Gandhi. They prayed that Gandhi would live through the night. The leader had refused to hide.

At sunrise Gandhi looked out at a shining blue sea. Practically from the moment he was up, people were snapping pictures of him. Gandhi brushed them away.

"Come," he said to his friends. Gandhi walked to the water's edge. He slowly bent down. And between two fingers he picked up a bit of salt. With this one small act, Gandhi flew in the face of the British Empire.

Within minutes, people all over India were making salt. Men, women and children rushed to the sea. They made salt in cups and buckets.

However, the police rushed in soon. They attacked on horses, swinging their sticks. Thousands of people were beaten or killed. Over 60,000 people were jailed for breaking the Salt Law. Yet not one Indian had raised a finger against the police. And Gandhi was still free.

He was living in a work camp near the sea. He had a small open house made of leaves. Each day he and the others in the camp made salt. At night Gandhi led meetings.

"Papu," one of his closest friends said. "Can I have a word with you?" Papu means father in Indian. Most of the people in his ashram called him Papu.

"Yes, but be quick. It is time for evening prayer meeting," Gandhi said. He looked tired.

"That's what I want to speak to you about. I don't think you should continue to lead the meetings."

"Why ever not?"

"I am afraid for you. Thousands of people have been beaten and killed. Maybe you should lay low," said the friend.

"Don't be silly." Gandhi tried to move around his friend.

"Think of the people," the friend begged. "If we lose you, then what?"

"Have no fear," Gandhi replied. "I am a man of peace."

After prayer meeting that night everyone went to bed. Hardly anyone could sleep, though. The air was thick with danger. The police had become more and more violent. Several men sat up to keep watch. Only Gandhi was not troubled. He went right to sleep.

At midnight there was the sound of running horses. The men on watch jumped to their feet. Out of the darkness came 30 police, all carrying guns.

"Where's Gandhi?" one yelled, pulling back on his horse. "Where's he hiding?"

Hadn't they learned anything yet? Gandhi never hid. And he always went to jail peacefully. Why 30 police? Why the guns?

Someone pointed to Gandhi's little open house. He was there, sleeping soundly as a baby.

One policeman shined a flashlight in his face. "Come with us Mr. Mohandas K. Gandhi. We will give you the time to get your things together."

"I am ready now," said Gandhi sleepily. He pointed to himself. "These are my things."

"Then come on."

"Ah! One second," he said. He went to his wash bowl. The great leader brushed his one or two teeth. He turned with a big smile for the police. Then he said, "Okay, let's go."

Back in jail again, Gandhi made good use of his time. He sent letters to people telling them how to carry on his work. He felt at home there. In fact, one time a man had asked for his home address. This was at a time when Gandhi was *not* in jail. But he gave the man the jail address.

The people continued fighting the Salt Law long after Gandhi was thrown in jail. Finally, the British were getting the point—blows to the head were no match for *soul force*. The Indian people were on a longer march than the Salt March. They were on the march for independence. And they would keep on marching or die.

13

Independence is Close at Hand

At last the British were ready (really, forced) to talk. A man named Lord Irwin was now the British head of India. He was going to London to meet with English leaders. They planned on talking about Indian independence. The talks would be called the Round Table talks.

Lord Irwin invited a few Indians to join the talks. These Indians were rich princes. They were doing very well under English rule.

At the last minute Lord Irwin had second thoughts. "Do you think I should invite Gandhi to the Round Table talks?" he asked a friend in the government.

"My Lord," the man answered. "If you do not invite Gandhi, you have not invited India. Gandhi *is* India."

Lord Irwin felt a little silly. The invitation was to meet with the top men in the British Empire. Should he send one to an old man in jail? But Lord Irwin invited Gandhi, just the same.

Gandhi was let out of jail. He sailed for England. He had not been there since his school days.

Gandhi took a live goat on the ship with him. He milked the goat every day for his meals. People were used to the strange man by now. He could get away with anything.

Gandhi had been invited to stay in King George's palace. Instead, he stayed in the poorest part of town. Each morning he took long walks through the streets of London. Children ran after the old man laughing. "Where are your pants, Gandhi?"

Each day he went to meetings at the palace. He wore only his homespun. Once a newspaper writer asked him, "Don't you think you're a little underdressed for the king's palace?"

"Oh, no," Gandhi answered. "King George is wearing enough clothes for us both."

The Round Table meeting did not come to much. All different groups were there. And each one wanted something different for India. Many of them wanted different rights for different groups of people.

Gandhi sat with his eyes closed through all of the talks. He didn't say much. No one knows what he was thinking. Maybe he was wondering why he had gotten talked into politics again. In any case, he wasn't happy.

He would not hear of a divided India. All people in free India must be equal—or it would not be "free." But at the Round Table, Gandhi was alone in this belief.

He went home very disappointed. Then, once again, he was thrown in jail. No one said why.

In 1932 Gandhi went back to the work he loved. He walked among the villages of India teaching the power of *soul force*. He fought against untouchability with his teaching. He set up schools.

Independence was sure to come soon. The only question was when and how. But people's attention had turned on other things for a while. The shadow of war hung over the world. Hitler was on the march in Europe. And in 1939 World War Two broke out.

Britain went to war. And so, of course, they pulled India along as well. Some Indian leaders wanted to strike a deal with Britain. India would help fight the war—if the country got independence afterwards.

Winston Churchill was now head of Great Britain. He was not friendly to the idea of India's independence. He said he was head of "the greatest country in the world." And he wasn't going to watch it fall apart.

Churchill did not like Gandhi. That was okay with Gandhi. He no longer wanted to help the British. And he thought they didn't need to make a deal. Independence was around the corner, whether Winston Churchill liked it or not.

However, new problems were coming up in India. A new leader of the Muslim people had come to power. His name was Mohammed Ali Jinnah. This man did not want to work with Gandhi and the other Indian leaders. He did not trust them. He did not believe they would protect the rights of the Muslim people.

"There must be two countries," he said, his mouth a tight line. "When India is free, we will make it two countries. One for the Hindus and one for the Muslims."

"But don't you see?" Gandhi asked him. "Hindus and Muslims have lived side by side for thousands of years."

"And there has always been fighting," snapped Jinnah.

"Yes, but you are causing more of it. As leaders it is not our job to set groups against one another. We must work to put out the fire of hate—not to build it up."

"I'm afraid we do not see eye to eye," Jinnah answered flatly.

Jinnah's idea took hold among Hindus and Muslims alike. Two countries sounded like a good plan. The two groups were fighting more and more. Violence broke out daily in the streets. Hindus were killing Muslims. Muslims were killing Hindus.

Gandhi was very, very sad. What did he care about independence if it brought such hatred? The country was close to independence, but that meant nothing to Gandhi now. Not with so much killing. Not if India was going to be divided.

Then Gandhi was once again thrown in jail. This time it was for saying he was against India going into World War Two. Kasturbai went to jail with him.

Then, as if his sadness over India were not enough, Kasturbai died. She had been by his side since he was 13. She had helped him in his work. She had gone to jail with him many times. By now, she was like a part of his body. In their last years they had hardly ever talked. She had not always understood the ideas of her learned husband. Yet she had always been there by his side.

Gandhi became sick himself at the time of Kasturbai's death. Once again everyone worried whether Gandhi would pull through. He got well, though. And the British set him free.

Gandhi knew he must overcome his sadness. There was much work to be done.

He had to stop the bloody fighting all over India. He tried to talk with Jinnah once more. But Jinnah was a man who liked his power. Many said he wanted a country of his own to rule. And that was why he wanted India divided.

Gandhi tried to offer him everything. He even said Jinnah could rule all of India. Anything to keep the country as one. But Jinnah looked hard at Gandhi. He did not trust the offer. It must be a trick. No, he wanted his own country to rule. It would be a country for Muslims. And it would be called Pakistan.

14

The Fast Unto Death

On August 15, 1947, full independence was given to India and Pakistan. Jinnah had gotten his country. Nehru was leader of India.

The sad part was that instead of having parties in the streets, people were fighting. For Muslims and Hindus lived together in towns all over India and Pakistan. The Hindus in Pakistan all were moving to India. And the Muslims in India all were moving to Pakistan.

No one really wanted to leave their homes. Yet people were packing up everything. Many of them were very angry. A war broke out along the line between the two countries.

Gandhi was 78 years old now. He set out to stop the fighting. He headed straight for the most dangerous places where small wars were breaking out. He walked right into the middle of the fights. He stood bare-footed and held up his hands. Soon the people quieted down.

Many people didn't want to listen to the old man anymore. Their lives were in an uproar. They were angry. Who was this old man talking about Muslims and Hindus living in peace? Couldn't he see it was too late for that?

His loved ones begged him to stay home. There were now more people than ever who wanted him dead. Still he held his evening prayer meetings. And he walked everywhere in the open. He went barefoot and without police protection.

And believe it or not, the old man still had his power. If people talked against him behind his back, to his face they grew ashamed. In every town he went, he stopped the fighting. Everywhere people promised him they would live in peace. After Gandhi quieted the people in one town, he would march to the next.

Finally, he arrived in Delhi, a very big city.

The fighting there was too much for him. He could not stop their anger.

"I will fast," Gandhi told his friends. "What good have the 78 years of my life been if people still act like this? I will fast unto my death—or until the fighting stops. Whichever comes first."

The war between the Hindus and Muslims had gotten out of hand. Neither group wanted to stop. Gandhi lay fasting in a house in Delhi. Through his open window, he heard the fighting below. "Let Gandhi die!" someone screamed.

Some Hindus were mad at Gandhi. They didn't want peace with Muslims. They were angry the Muslims were taking away part of their country. Gandhi was wrong to talk about peace with them. It was time for war.

People threw rocks at Gandhi's house. They sent him hateful letters. Sure he used to be great. But his ideas were now outdated. Some said, "Why didn't the old man die on the day of independence?"

Meanwhile, Nehru rushed to Delhi. He must see Gandhi. He must talk him out of this fasting madness. Many other Indian leaders were already at Gandhi's bedside.

Nehru pushed through the people in the streets near the house where Gandhi lay. He ran up the steps. People were yelling.

"Let Gandhi die!" someone shouted again. Nehru stopped in his tracks. He swung around.

"Who said that?" he screamed. "Come forth! I ask you, who said that?" Nehru's eyes flashed anger.

A man with him took Nehru's arm. "Come on, we must go to Papu."

"Yes," he said. They went to Gandhi's bedside. "Papu," Nehru said taking his hand. "The fighting has quieted down in many parts of the city. Please eat something. India needs you. We all need you."

Gandhi turned to look at his friend, now the leader of India. He could hardly open his eyes. The nurse whispered something to Nehru. Gandhi was going to die very soon.

"I . . . will . . . not . . . eat." Gandhi forced the words out. He could hardly whisper. "Until there . . . is . . . no . . . fighting."

Just then a man ran in. He had been crying.

His eyes were red and puffy. The Hindu man dropped to his knees beside Gandhi.

"Papu," he started. "I have come to you for forgiveness. I have killed a Muslim baby."

"But why?" Gandhi asked.

"They killed my son—my only son!" The man broke down. He cried into his hands. He was shaking all over. "Oh, what will I do?"

"That . . . is . . . easy," whispered the dying man. "Go find a Muslim baby. Find one whose parents have been killed. Take the child into your own home. Raise him as you would your son."

The man backed off shaking his head. "I will," he said over and over. "I will, I will." Then he ran out.

"Don't you see, Papu," Nehru said. "The people want you to live. All over the country Hindus are making up with their Muslim brothers and sisters."

Just then a girl ran in.

"Papu! Papu!" she cried. "It has stopped. Listen to me. All over India, Muslims and Hindus are praying for you—they are praying *together."*

Could it be true? People who were trying to kill each other only yesterday are praying together today?

"It is true," Nehru said. "Listen." He threw the window open even wider. The streets were quiet. "There is no one fighting now, Papu. Not one Hindu. Not one Muslim."

Gandhi looked around his bed. All the great Indian leaders were there—Hindu and Muslim alike. All promised to keep the peace. They promised to live together as brothers.

One old man had stopped a war by refusing to eat.

Gandhi turned to the young woman who was his nurse. The old man smiled as he asked, "Would you please bring me a glass of orange juice? I believe it is time for a bite to eat."

15

Evening Prayers in the Garden

With one fast Gandhi had brought peace to India and Pakistan. He ate slowly and just a little for the first two or three days. At 78 it took time to get strong again.

Nehru knew India needed Gandhi. For there were still many who did not want peace. There were Hindus who wanted to go to war with Pakistan. Like Gandhi, they thought India and Pakistan should be one country. Unlike Gandhi, they thought war was the answer to the problem. A man named Godse was one such Hindu.

Twelve days after his fast ended, Gandhi was walking to evening prayers. He was still weak. Two young girls were helping him walk.

He reached the garden. He was moving through the people to the front. Suddenly a man showed up before him. The man fell to his knees. Gandhi blessed him. The man's name was Godse.

In the next minute, Godse pulled out his gun. And he shot one of the greatest leaders the world has ever known.

Godse killed Gandhi because he wanted war with Pakistan. He knew that as long as Gandhi lived, there would be peace. Godse believed the death of Gandhi would cause a war to break out.

In fact, it did just the opposite. Muslims and Hindus all over India and Pakistan joined together in their sorrow. Together they prayed. And in his name they promised to try and live peacefully.

Gandhi knew that some day he would be killed. He also knew that no one could kill what he stood for. And he was right. All over the world today people are using *soul force* and nonviolent action to make change. Martin Luther King used these ideas in the 1960's in America. People have learned that you cannot fight violence with more violence. They have learned from Mahatma Gandhi that true revolution must happen in the hearts of men and women.